D0337838

FLAVOURS SERIES

Salmon

Elaine Elliot & Virginia Lee

Formac Publishing Company Limited
Halifax

In continuing the theme of the Flavours series of cookbooks, we have invited chefs from across Canada to share their recipes, and we thank them for their generosity. Each recipe has been tested and adjusted for the home cook.   *– Elaine Elliot and Virginia Lee*

Special thanks to **Craig Flinn**, chef and proprietor of Chives Canadian Bistro in Halifax, for preparing and styling many of the recipes photographed for this book.

Participating restaurants

British Columbia
A Snug Harbour Inn, Ucluelet, BC
The Aerie Resort, Malahat, BC
Bishop's Restaurant, Vancouver, BC
The Doorknocker Bed and Breakfast, Richmond, BC
Horizons Restaurant, Vancouver, BC
Nautical Nellies Steak & Seafood House, Victoria, BC
Val d'Isère Restaurant, Whistler, BC

Alberta
Pyramid Lake Resort, Jasper, AB
River House Grill, St. Albert, AB

Manitoba
The Current Restaurant at Inn at the Forks, Winnipeg, MB

Ontario
Deerhurst Resort, Huntsville, ON
The Epicurean Restaurant & Bistro,
    Niagara-on-the-Lake, ON
Inn on the Twenty, Jordan, ON
Keefer Mansion Inn, Thorold, ON
Ste. Anne's Resort and Spa, Grafton, ON
Vineland Estates Winery Restaurant, Vineland, ON
Wellington Court Restaurant, St. Catharines, ON

Quebec
L'Orée du Bois, Chelsea, QC
Restaurant Les Fougères, Chelsea, QC

New Brunswick
Inn on the Cove and Spa, Saint John, NB
Little Shemogue Country Inn, Little Shemogue, NB
Marshlands Inn, Sackville, NB
Quaco Inn, St. Martins, NB
Dufferin Inn & San Martello Dining Room, Saint John, NB

Prince Edward Island
Dalvay by the Sea, Dalvay, PE
The Dunes Café and Gardens, Brackley Beach, PE
Inn at Bay Fortune, Bay Fortune, PE
Shaws Hotel, Brackley Beach, PE

Nova Scotia
Acton's Grill & Café, Wolfville, NS
The Blomidon Inn, Wolfville, NS
Da Maurizio Dining Room, Halifax, NS
Inn on the Lake, Waverley, NS
Keltic Lodge Resort and Spa, Ingonish Beach, NS
La Perla, Dartmouth, NS
The Markland Coastal Resort, Dingwall, NS
The Normaway Inn, Margaree Valley, NS
The Pines Resort, Digby, NS
Stories at Halliburton House Inn, Halifax, NS
Sweet Basil Bistro, Halifax, NS

For Library and Archives Canada Cataloguing in Publication information, see p. 96

Copyright © 2007 Formac Publishing Company
All rights reserved. No part of this book may be reproduced or transmitted in any form or by any means, electronic or mechanical, including photocopying, or by any information storage or retrieval system, without permission in writing from the publisher.

Formac Publishing Company Limited recognizes the support of the Province of Nova Scotia through the Department of Tourism, Culture and Heritage. We acknowledge the financial support of the Government of Canada through the Book Publishing Industry Development Program (BPIDP) for our publishing activities.

Formac Publishing Company Limited
5502 Atlantic Street
Halifax, Nova Scotia B3H 1G4
www.formac.ca

Printed and bound in Canada

Contents

Introduction

Depending upon where you live, you will find different species of salmon available in fish markets, at the seafood department of local grocery stores or in restaurants. The recipes in this collection have been gathered from chefs across Canada, highlighting their personal preferences of this delightful fish, but you can substitute whichever salmon species is available in your area, or the one most pleasing to your palate.

Salmon Varieties

Atlantic

Atlantic Salmon, *Salmo salar,* is the only salmon native to north Atlantic waters and its freshwater tributaries. Its range once extended from New York's Hudson River, along the coast of the north Atlantic to Russia's White Sea and down past Scotland and Ireland as far as Portugal. Stocks are now severely depleted, and many of the historic runs of this species are reduced or extinct. Today the wild Atlantic salmon is considered endangered. In the wild, a mature Atlantic salmon will average 10 lb (5 kg), making it a prize to sports fishermen, who ideally practice a "catch and release" policy.

Aquaculture studies in the 1980s perfected a way to farm or pen-raise Atlantic salmon and it continues to be a very popular food fish. It is farmed in cold Atlantic waters from Norway, Scotland and Ireland to eastern Canada — primarily New Brunswick and Nova Scotia. In addition, this species is farmed in Pacific waters by Canada, the United States and Chile. In fact, as a species, it accounts for more than 80 percent of the world's farm-raised salmon.

Farmed Atlantic salmon are harvested at 4 to 5 lb (2 to 2.5 kg). Available year-round, they are similar to the Pacific king or Chinook salmon in oil content, with bright pink flesh. They are sleek with steel-blue backs covered with black crosses and silver to white bellies.

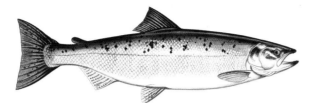

King / Chinook

King or chinook salmon, *Oncorhynchus tshawytscha,* is the largest of the five main salmon species inhabiting Pacific waters. It ranges from central California north to Alaska's Yukon River. Kings account for less than 5 percent of harvested salmon. They have the highest oil content and are the most expensive. Wild kings, which average between 16 and 24 lb (8 to 12 kg), are available fresh in the spring and through September, with small quantities being taken in the winter.

Farmers raise smaller kings, usually between 4 and 7 lb (2 to 3.5 kg), which are available year round. Kings are blue-green on their backs with silver and white bellies. They have black spots on their upper half and distinctive black gums. The flesh ranges in colour from prized white to pinkish-red.

Coho / Silver

Coho or silver salmon, *Oncorhynchus kisutch,* is close to king salmon in flavour but smaller in size, and the species makes up less than 5 percent of the North American catch. It ranges from Oregon to Alaska's Bering Sea, and is also found in some freshwater areas, including the Great Lakes. Averaging 10 lb (5 kg) this fish has a bright red flesh colour. Adults in the ocean have steel blue to slightly green backs with small black spots, silvery sides and white gums and bellies.

Fresh wild coho are available from July to September, with August being the peak season.

Coho are farmed, mainly in Chile for export to Japan, and sold at about 1 lb (0.5 kg).

Sockeye / Red

Sockeye or red salmon, *Oncorhynchus nerka*, is the most valuable commercially harvested Pacific salmon. Caught during the summer months from Washington's Puget Sound to Alaska's Bristol Bay, the catch is sold fresh, frozen for export or canned. Sockeyes average 6 lb (3 kg) and are high in oil content. They have the reddest flesh of any salmon. There is an abundant supply of this species and it is not farmed.

A non-anadromous type of sockeye is the *kokanee*, a land-locked dweller in freshwater lakes and streams. It is found from California to Alaska, Idaho and even in Japan. These fish are similar to sockeye although smaller in length and weight. They are brilliant steel blue to green-blue with no distinctive spots and with bright red flesh. Kokanee are excellent sport fish, taking both flies and lures.

Chum / Dog / Keta

Chum, dog or keta salmon, *Oncorhynchus keta*, at an average 8 lb (4 kg) is quite similar to Coho or silver salmon, although it has paler flesh and lower oil content, which makes it less desirable for marketing purposes. Chums are not farmed.

Pink / Humpback

Pink or humpback salmon, *Oncorhynchus gorbuscha*, is the smallest of the Pacific salmon. Averaging 4 lb (2 kg) these salmon are abundant and are not farmed. Pinks account for almost half the West Coast salmon landings, but with their pale pink flesh and slightly lower oil content, they are generally canned.

Wild Versus Farmed Salmon

For centuries, salmon was an abundant food source throughout Europe and North America. Slowly, with industrialization, rivers became polluted and dams were built for hydro projects, altering the natural course of rivers. These environmental changes plus overfishing have greatly diminished stocks of wild salmon. One response to this situation is to farm salmon. Salmon farms have produced mixed results: we now have plentiful and inexpensive sources of Atlantic salmon, but farming methods can result in contamination of surrounding waters. Farmed salmon often escape and introduce diseases and parasites to wild salmon — problems that can be treated when the fish are in farms, but not in the wild.

Fortunately there are other options for people concerned about the problems caused by salmon farming. Wild Pacific or BC salmon is a good alternative to farmed Atlantic salmon. Be sure to ask what type of salmon your fishmonger is selling and where it was caught, as certain fish may be plentiful in one area but severely depleted in another. Many websites, such as Sustainable Seafood Canada (www.seachoice.org), are devoted to sustainable seafood choices.

Nutritional Value

Salmon is rich in Omega-3 polyunsaturated fatty acids, which significantly lower blood triglycerides and cholesterol levels. It contains vitamins A, C and E as well as niacin and riboflavin. Vitamins C and E are powerful antioxidants. It is purported that diets containing fish once a week reduce the likelihood of developing dementia. A 6-oz (170-g) serving of Atlantic salmon contains 272 calories.

Buying and Storing Salmon

Fresh salmon is extremely perishable so it is important to know how to check for freshness. The fish should have a slightly sweet odour, bright scales and red gills. The eyes should be clear and slightly bulging and the flesh should bounce back when lightly touched.

When buying fillets or steaks look for firm, moist flesh that is a bright colour. Avoid fish that is blemished or dry around the edges. Find a good fish market and build a rapport with the fishmonger; he or she will be able to offer excellent advice.

When buying frozen salmon look for solid product with no dry spots or edges. It should be properly wrapped and have an ice glaze, but no frost or freezer burn.

As fresh salmon deteriorates rapidly it is best to prepare the fish within hours of purchase. If that is not possible, rinse the fish in cold water to which you have added a few drops of lemon juice. Pat dry and store in an airtight container in the coldest section of your refrigerator for *no longer than 2 days*.

Store frozen salmon in a freezer for *no longer than 2 to 3 months*. If the fish thaws, do not refreeze.

Preparation

To prepare salmon successfully and to preserve its texture it is essential to avoid overcooking. The rule of thumb is to measure the fish at its thickest section and cook it for 10 minutes per inch of thickness (5 to 7 minutes per cm). This rule is reliable and applies to steaks, fillets or whole fish, whether baking, broiling, grilling, poaching or frying. For microwave cooking, cook 3 to 5 minutes per pound of fish (6 to 10 minutes per kg) in a 700-watt oven, or follow the manufacturer's directions.

To test for doneness, insert a knife into the thickest part; the juices should run clear and the flesh should be opaque, moist and flake easily.

Smoked Salmon Crêpes, p.22

Appetizers

Salmon is oh-so-much more than a sandwich ingredient! In this section our contributing chefs have provided delectable dishes using this beautiful pink fish. Be sure to try the Two Salmon Tartare from L'Orée du Bois in Chelsea, Quebec — an eye appealing spread packed full of flavour — or treat yourself to the Smoked Salmon Appetizer Plate, a speciality of Wolfville's Blomidon Inn.

Marinated Atlantic Salmon
with a Trio of Peppercorns

Stories at Halliburton House Inn, Halifax, NS

Chef Maurice Pohl at the Halliburton House Inn allows the action of the acid in the lemon juice to "cook" the salmon in this flavourful appetizer. Fish prepared in this manner is called ceviche, and only the freshest or sushi grade seafood should be used. In his presentation he relies upon colour contrasts using tri-coloured peppercorns with yellow lemon and green lime slices.

1 ½ tsp (7 mL) each of dried green, pink and
   black peppercorns
⅓ cup (75 mL) fresh lemon juice
2 tsp (10 mL) coarse sea salt
⅓ cup (75 mL) olive oil
1 lb (500 g) fresh salmon, sliced ¼-in (0.5-cm)
   thick
lemon and lime slices
fresh parsley and rosemary

Coarsely grind peppercorns in a peppermill or crush with a mortar and pestle; place in a small bowl. Gradually whisk lemon juice, salt and olive oil into peppercorns and spoon half of the mixture over the bottom of a non-metallic platter. Spread salmon evenly on marinade and cover with remaining mixture. Cover and refrigerate 2 to 3 hours.

To serve: carefully remove salmon from marinade and arrange on serving dish. Garnish with lemon wedges and fresh herbs. Accompany with toast points, crackers or fresh bread.

Serves 4 to 6.

Two Salmon
Tartare

L'Orée du Bois, Chelsea, QC

This spread featuring both fresh and smoked salmon flavoured with capers and fresh herbs makes a wonderful hors d'oeuvre or first course dish. Since the non-smoked salmon is served "raw," use only very fresh salmon of the highest quality.

6 oz (170 g) fresh salmon
6 oz (170 g) smoked salmon
1 ½ tbsp (22 mL) minced shallot
1 tbsp (15 mL) chopped fresh herbs (tarragon, parsley, chives)
1 tbsp (15 mL) drained capers, chopped
2 tsp (10 mL) fresh lime juice
3 ½ tbsp (52 mL) mayonnaise
3 to 4 drops Tabasco sauce
salt and pepper

Remove bones and skin from salmon and cut both kinds into tiny cubes using a very sharp knife. In a bowl, add all ingredients except salt and pepper; mix to combine. Adjust seasoning with salt and pepper and extra Tabasco and lime juice if desired. Cover and refrigerate.

To serve: remove from refrigerator 15 minutes before serving. Accompany with crostini rye bread or crackers of choice.

Makes 1 ½ cups (375 mL).

Smoked Salmon
Quiches

These tasty little quiches are designed to be served as an opener before the main meal or as part of an hors d'oeuvre offering at a larger gathering. They are easy to make and can be prepared in advance. To reheat, simply pop in a 350°F (180°C) oven until heated through.

12 small, unbaked pastry shells
2 tbsp (30 mL) unsalted butter
½ cup (125 mL) finely chopped button
   mushrooms
1 green onion, thinly sliced
1 egg, beaten
⅓ cup (75 mL) sour cream
4 oz (120 g) smoked salmon, diced

Preheat oven to 375°F (190°C). Place pastry shells on a baking sheet.

Heat butter in a skillet over medium-high heat; add mushrooms and onion and sauté until tender, about 3 minutes. Remove from heat and cool slightly.

In a small bowl combine egg, sour cream and mushroom mixture. Divide salmon between pastry shells; top with egg mixture. Bake until golden, about 25 minutes. Serve warm.

Makes 12 tarts.

Smoked Salmon
Appetizer Plate

The Blomidon Inn, Wolfville, NS

There are several ways to prepare smoked salmon and at the Blomidon Inn the chef prefers the "cold method," where Atlantic salmon is processed in a smoke house at temperatures between 20 and 27°C (70 and 80°F) from 24 hours up to several days. The results are somewhat similar to gravlax or Danish-smoked salmon. This delicacy is served paper-thin, accompanied by capers.

mixed salad greens
12 oz (350 g) cold-smoked salmon, thinly sliced
1 red onion, thinly sliced
2 tbsp (30 mL) capers
Cream Cheese Chantilly (recipe follows)
4 to 6 lemon wedges
Melba Toast (recipe follows)

To serve: on a large dinner plate place a few pieces of salad greens at the top of the plate. Fan out 2 to 3 oz (60 to 90 g) of smoked salmon. Place 5 or 6 rings of red onion and the capers over the smoked salmon. Drizzle Cream Cheese Chantilly over the smoked salmon and onion. Garnish with pieces of Melba toast and lemon wedges.

Serves 4 to 6.

Cream Cheese Chantilly
½ cup (125 mL) cream cheese, softened
¼ cup (60 mL) sour cream
¼ cup (60 mL) mayonnaise
light cream (10% m.f.)

Blend together cream cheese, sour cream and mayonnaise. Add enough cream to reach a pouring consistency.

Makes 1 cup (250 mL).

Melba Toast

Cut a baguette on an angle in 1⁄4-in (0.5-cm) slices. Spread with garlic butter and toast in a preheated 350°F (180°C) oven until lightly golden. Cool.

Bourbon-Laced Grilled Atlantic Salmon
Cream Cheese Spread

Keltic Lodge, Ingonish Beach, NS

Executive Chef Dale Nichols finds that bourbon whiskey and honey give a nice flavour edge to this delicious cream spread. In addition to crackers, Chef Nichols also serves the spread with mini savoury pancakes or rolled up in a tortilla.

10 oz (280 g) salmon fillet
3 tbsp (45 mL) vegetable oil, divided
salt and pepper
1 tsp (5 mL) caraway seeds
1 tsp (5 mL) celery seeds
½ cup (125 mL) diced onion
2 tbsp (30 mL) bourbon whiskey
1 tsp (5 mL) honey
8 oz (225 g) cream cheese, softened
salt and pepper, second amount
2 tbsp (30 mL) chopped parsley
2 tbsp (30 mL) finely diced red pepper

Preheat grill to medium high. Brush salmon with 2 tbsp (30 mL) oil and season with salt and pepper. Grill salmon until cooked through.

Remove from grill, break up into small pieces and reserve to cool.

Heat a skillet over medium-high heat; add caraway and celery seeds and toast, stirring frequently, 2 to 3 minutes. Add remaining vegetable oil and onion to skillet and sauté until onion is cooked and golden on the edges. Deglaze skillet with whiskey and honey and cook until liquid is reduced to one-quarter. Cool mixture slightly. Add mixture to a food processor and purée.

In a mixing bowl, combine cream cheese and onion mixture and stir to blend. Fold in salmon, parsley and red pepper. Adjust seasoning with salt and pepper and spoon into serving dish.

To serve: accompany with crackers or crostini.

Makes 1 ½ cups (375 mL).

Dill-Cured Salmon Platter
with Seasoned Greens

The Epicurean Restaurant & Bistro, Niagara-on-the-Lake, ON

Curing your own salmon gives much the same pleasure as baking fresh bread, finishing a large project or creating a masterpiece; you cannot believe that you have actually made something so wonderful. And the pièce de résistance is that the process is so simple!

Salmon
1 lb (500 g) boneless salmon fillet, with skin
⅓ cup (75 mL) chopped fresh dill
¼ cup (60 mL) sea salt
¼ cup (60 mL) sugar
freshly ground pepper

Remove all bones from salmon (this is easily done with a pair of clean tweezers) and lay fillet, skin side down, on a rimmed baking sheet that has been lined with plastic wrap.

Combine dill, salt and sugar in a food processor and pulse until most of the dill is broken down.

Generously grind pepper over salmon and cover with the dill mixture, coating evenly. Wrap the salmon in the plastic wrap. Keeping it on the baking sheet, refrigerate 2 days (3 days for larger fillets) turning occasionally.

With cold water, gently wash the dill mixture off the fish and pat dry. Rinse and dry the baking sheet. Place fillet on baking sheet, skin side down, and return to refrigerator to dry, up to 1 day.

Slice the salmon as thinly as possible on the bias with a sharp, thin-bladed knife, leaving the skin behind.

Greens
1 head blond frisée
chives
salt and pepper

Separate frisée leaves; wash and dry. Cut chives into 2-in (5-cm) lengths. Reserve.

Vinaigrette
2 tbsp (30 mL) sherry vinegar
3 tbsp (45 mL) grape seed oil
3 tbsp (45 mL) walnut oil

In a bowl, whisk together vinegar and oils until emulsified. Makes ½ cup (125 mL).

To serve: on a large tray or serving dish, make a mound with the greens and drizzle with the vinaigrette. Layer the salmon slices around the greens and sprinkle with chives, salt and pepper. Serve with individual appetizer plates and small forks.

Serves 6 to 8.

Salmon
Roll

Serve yourself — what could be easier for the busy host or hostess? The surprising addition of horseradish gives bite to this appetizer, and we suggest preparing it a day in advance, allowing the flavours to blend and the log to become firm.

7 ½ oz (213 g) tin sockeye or coho salmon
8 oz (250 g) cream cheese, softened
1 tbsp (15 mL) lemon juice
2 tbsp (30 mL) minced onion
1 tbsp (15 mL) creamed horseradish
¼ tsp (1 mL) salt
½ cup (125 mL) chopped walnuts or pecans
3 tbsp (45 mL) chopped parsley

Drain salmon, remove skin and bones and flake with a fork. In a food processor combine cream cheese, lemon juice, onion, horseradish and salt. Pulse until blended. Add salmon to bowl and pulse until just combined. Refrigerate 30 minutes.

Form cheese mixture into a log and roll in chopped nuts and parsley until coated. Wrap in plastic wrap and refrigerate at least 24 hours.

To serve: accompany with assorted crackers.

Makes 1 roll.

Smoked Salmon
Crêpes

The Doorknocker Bed and Breakfast, Richmond, BC

Innkeeper Jeanette Jarville notes that these crêpes may be prepared in advance of serving. Simply store separated with waxed paper in a covered container in refrigerator up to three days or freeze up to one month.

2 cups (500 mL) whole milk (3.5 % m.f.)
4 eggs
¼ cup (60 mL) melted butter
2 cups (500 mL) all-purpose flour
vegetable spray for crêpe pan
Smoked Salmon Filling (recipe follows)

Blend milk, eggs, butter and flour in a blender until smooth. Stop blender and scrape down sides as necessary. Add a little more milk if batter appears too thick — it should pour easily. Allow batter to rest 30 minutes. Heat crêpe pan over medium high heat and coat with vegetable spray. Pour 2 tablespoons (30 mL) batter into centre of pan and swirl to form an 8-in (20-cm) crêpe. Cook crêpe until lightly browned, about 1 minute; flip and cook other side. Remove and set aside. Repeat process, spraying with oil as necessary. Separate crêpes with waxed paper and refrigerate in a covered container.

Smoked Salmon Filling
8 oz (225 g) cream cheese, softened
⅓ cup (75 mL) sour cream
½ tsp (2 mL) finely chopped dill
4 oz (120 g) smoked wild BC salmon, diced
salt and pepper
thin cucumber slices, smoked salmon slivers, dill sprigs and capers as garnish

Preheat oven to 350°F (180°C). Using a mixer, blend together the cheese, sour cream and dill. Fold in smoked salmon and adjust seasoning with salt and pepper.

Spread approximately 2 tablespoons (30 mL) cheese filling in a line down the centre of each crêpe. Roll and place on a cookie sheet, seam side down. Bake, loosely covered with aluminum foil, 20 to 25 minutes, until crêpes are warm and slightly puffed.

To serve: arrange two crêpes on a plate. Garnish, if desired, with thin cucumber slices, smoked salmon slivers, dill sprigs and capers.

Makes 14 to 16 crêpes.

Quenelles of Fresh Atlantic Salmon
with Lemon Chive Cream

Acton's Grill & Café, Wolfville, NS

We suggest you prepare this delicate dish just before serving time. It makes a wonderful first course to a special dinner but also works well as a luncheon or main course entrée — just increase the portion.

8 oz (225 g) fresh salmon, boned and skinned, cut into small pieces
2 egg whites
¾ cup (175 mL) heavy cream (35% m.f.)
1 tbsp (15 mL) fresh dill, chopped
1 tbsp (15 mL) fresh lemon juice
pinch cayenne pepper
salt and freshly ground white pepper
Poaching Liquid (recipe follows)
Lemon Chive Cream (recipe follows)

In a food processor, place salmon pieces and egg whites; purée until smooth, about 1 minute. Add cream and process 20 seconds longer. Remove mixture to a bowl and gently fold in dill, lemon juice and cayenne pepper. Season with salt and pepper. Cover and refrigerate at least 30 minutes.

Poaching Liquid:
1 small carrot, peeled and diced
2 stalks celery, diced
1 medium onion, diced
1 large bay leaf
1 tsp (5 mL) white peppercorns
4 whole cloves
2 cups (500 mL) dry white wine
6 cups (1.5 L) water
salt

In a large saucepan, combine all ingredients except the salt and bring to a boil. Reduce heat and simmer, covered, 30 minutes. Strain liquid into another saucepan, season with salt and reheat to simmer.

Remove quenelle mixture from refrigerator. With a tablespoon, form quenelles to the size of small walnuts. Drop portions into the simmering liquid and poach for 8 minutes, making sure that the poaching liquid does not boil. Quenelles will rise to the top when cooked. Remove with a slotted spoon onto a serving dish and keep warm.

To serve: creatively arrange quenelles on each plate and nap with Lemon Chive Cream. Garnish with chopped parsley.

Serves 6.

Lemon Chive Cream
1 tbsp (15 mL) butter
1 shallot, finely diced
1 cup (250 mL) dry white wine
juice of 1 lemon
2 cups (500 mL) heavy cream (35% m.f.)
¼ cup (60 mL) chopped chives
salt and white pepper

Heat butter in a saucepan over low heat; add
shallot and cook, stirring frequently until
softened, about 5 minutes. Add wine and
lemon juice; bring to a boil and reduce by half.
Add cream and reduce until slightly thickened.
Remove from heat and stir in chives. Adjust
seasoning with salt and pepper. Keep warm.

Gravlax Salad with Papaya Basil Salsa, p.36

Soups and Salads

The offering of either a soup or chilled salad can be the prelude to a great dining experience. Several of the recipes in this collection would, however, make a satisfying luncheon course on their own. Keefer Mansion Inn's Oat-Crusted Salmon on Wild Blueberry, Frisée and Spinach Salad or The Current Restaurant's Open Sesame Salmon with Zucchini Ribbon Salad are substantial, yet very pleasing to the eye.

Salmon
Bisque

The Normaway Inn, Margaree Valley, NS

Although bisques are traditionally puréed, this version from David MacDonald, owner/chef of The Normaway Inn, is presented with flaked salmon. The flavour is obtained by using some of the poaching liquid in which the salmon has been cooked. For a lower-fat version, we tested the recipe using two cups of milk instead of the milk-light cream combination, and while not as rich, the taste was not compromised.

Poaching Liquid (recipe follows)
1 lb (500 g) salmon
¼ cup (60 mL) butter
¼ cup (60 mL) finely diced onion
¼ cup (60 mL) diced celery
3 tbsp (45 mL) all-purpose flour
1 cup (250 mL) light cream (10 % m.f.)
1 cup (250 mL) milk
1 cup (250 mL) tomato juice
2 tbsp (30 mL) chopped fresh parsley
salt and pepper

Add salmon to poaching liquid; poach until barely cooked. Remove salmon and cool slightly. Flake meat and reserve. Strain poaching liquid, reserving 1 cup for bisque.

Heat butter in a heavy-based saucepan over medium heat; add onion and celery and sauté, stirring frequently until softened, about 5 minutes. Add flour, stir to combine and cook 1 minute. Gently whisk light cream, milk and reserved poaching liquid into flour mixture and cook over moderate heat, stirring constantly, until smooth and thickened. Add tomato juice, parsley and flaked salmon; bring to serving temperature, being careful not to boil. Adjust seasoning with salt and pepper to taste.

To serve: ladle into warmed soup bowls.

Serves 4.

Poaching Liquid
2 cups (500 mL) water
¼ cup (60 mL) dry white wine
1 stalk celery with leaves, sliced
1 bay leaf
5 peppercorns

In a poaching pan, combine all ingredients and bring to a boil; reduce heat, cover and simmer 2 minutes.

Cape Breton
Fish Chowder

The Markland Coastal Resort, Dingwall, NS

True to Maritime tradition, we use ingredients that are readily at hand. Perched on the edge of the Atlantic, the chefs at Markland's have transformed salmon, large sea scallops and succulent Atlantic blue mussels in their shells into a chowder that shouts freshness.

¼ cup (60 mL) butter
3 potatoes, peeled and cubed
2 stalks celery, diced
1 carrot, diced
1 onion, diced
1 clove garlic, minced
¼ cup (60 mL) all-purpose flour
6 cups (1.5 L) seafood stock, portioned (optional chicken stock)
½ lb (250 g) skinless salmon fillet, cut in 1-in (2.5-cm) cubes
¼ lb (125 g) scallops, cut if large
1 lb (500 g) mussels, scrubbed and debearded
½ cup (125 mL) light cream (10% m.f.)
¼ cup (60 mL) heavy cream (35% m.f.)
4 tsp (20 mL) chopped fresh dill
4 tsp (20 mL) chopped fresh basil
salt and freshly ground pepper

In a large saucepan, melt butter over medium-high heat; sauté potatoes, celery, carrot, onion and garlic, stirring, 8 minutes or until softened. Stir in flour and gradually whisk in 5 cups (1.25 L) of stock. Bring to a boil, reduce heat and simmer, covered, until vegetables are tender, about 10 minutes.

Meanwhile in a separate saucepan, bring remaining stock to a boil. Reduce heat to simmer and poach salmon cubes for 1 minute; remove with slotted spoon and reserve. Poach scallops for 1 minute; remove with slotted spoon and reserve with salmon. Prepare mussels, being careful to remove any that have broken shells or do not close. Add mussels to stock, cover, and cook for 4 minutes or until they open. Remove mussels with a slotted spoon, discarding any that do not fully open; reserve with other seafood.

Strain poaching liquid into vegetable mixture; add light cream, heavy cream, dill and basil. Heat, being careful not to boil. Add reserved seafood. Adjust seasoning with salt and pepper and heat until steaming. Serve immediately.

Serves 6.

Marinated Salmon
Salad

The Pines Resort, Digby, NS

Only the freshest fish should be used in making this ceviche salad. The chemical action of fresh lime juice on the delicate salmon flesh "cooks" the seafood.

¼ cup (60 mL) fresh lime juice
6 tbsp (90 mL) extra virgin olive oil
6 drops Tabasco sauce
4 drops Worcestershire sauce
salt and freshly ground pepper
2 tbsp (30 mL) fresh herbs, chopped (dill, oregano, basil, etc.)
4 oz (120 g) salmon fillet
salad greens to serve 4
cherry tomatoes
asparagus spears, cooked and chilled

In a bowl whisk together lime juice, olive oil, Tabasco and Worcestershire sauces, salt, pepper and herbs until emulsified.

With a sharp knife, cut salmon in very thin slices and arrange on a shallow non-metallic platter. Brush one half of the vinaigrette evenly onto both sides of the salmon slices. Cover and reserve 5 minutes or until salmon is opaque and marinated.

To serve: toss remaining vinaigrette with salad greens and distribute on one side of 4 plates. Arrange marinated salmon on other side of plate. Garnish with cherry tomatoes and asparagus.

Serves 4.

Oat-Crusted Salmon on Wild Blueberry,
Frisée and Spinach Salad

The Keefer Mansion Inn, Thorold, ON

The crunchy honey-oat crust of this first-course salad or luncheon dish from Chef Bruce Worden tastes wonderful and makes an interesting presentation for guests. We found the Balsamic Reduction an ample seasoning for the greens, but feel free to serve vinaigrette on the side if you desire.

1 cup (250 mL) old-fashioned oat flakes
⅓ cup (60 mL) liquid honey
1 ½ lb (750 g) salmon fillet, with skin
1 tbsp (15 mL) vegetable oil
freshly ground pepper
½ cup (125 mL) fresh wild blueberries
1 medium red onion, thinly sliced
1 red pepper, roasted, peeled and julienned
3 cups (750 mL) blond frisée
3 cups (750 mL) spinach
Balsamic Reduction (recipe follows)

Preheat oven to 350°F (180°C).

In a bowl, combine oats and honey.

Cut salmon into 6 equal portions. Heat oil in a heavy ovenproof skillet over high heat. Add salmon, skin side down, and sear 2 minutes. Remove from heat and coat flesh sides of salmon with oat mixture, pressing to adhere.

Generously grind pepper over oat mixture. Remove to oven and bake until centre is just pink, about 6 minutes.

While salmon is baking, prepare salad. In a bowl combine blueberries, onion, red pepper, frisée and spinach; toss to combine.

To serve: divide salad among 6 plates, top with salmon and drizzle with Balsamic Reduction.

Serves 6 as a first course or 4 as a luncheon entrée.

Balsamic Reduction

1 cup (250 mL) balsamic vinegar
2 tbsp (30 mL) brown sugar

Heat vinegar in a small saucepan over medium-high heat; bring to a boil, stir frequently, and reduce by two-thirds. Towards the end of the reduction, add the brown sugar and stir to dissolve. Remove from heat. Cool. Reduction may be kept indefinitely in the refrigerator. Bring to room temperature before serving.

Makes ⅔ cup (150 mL).

Open Sesame Salmon
with Zucchini Ribbon Salad

The Current Restaurant at Inn at the Forks, Winnipeg, MB

Chef Barry Saunders notes that this item, one of the most popular on the menu, makes a wonderful summer meal any time of day. At the restaurant he uses a mandoline to slice his zucchini but notes that this can be accomplished using a sharp paring knife.

4 salmon fillets, 5 oz (140 g) each
½ cup (125 mL) pure maple syrup
1 cup (250 mL) low-sodium soy sauce
2 tbsp (30 mL) grated fresh ginger
2 tbsp (30 mL) combination black and white
  sesame seeds
1 tbsp (15 mL) olive oil
1 lime, cut into wedges
4 cilantro sprigs
Zucchini Ribbon Salad (recipe follows)

Rinse and pat dry salmon fillets. In a deep-sided dish combine maple syrup, soy sauce and fresh ginger. Marinate fillets, covered and refrigerated, at least 8 hours, turning several times.

Heat a non-stick skillet over medium heat and toast sesame seeds about 1 minute, shaking pan frequently. Set aside.

Remove salmon from marinade. Heat oil in a skillet over medium-high heat, add salmon and sear on both sides until nicely caramelised and cooked to desired doneness, about 4 minutes each side.

To serve: divide Zucchini Ribbon Salad between 4 plates. Top each salad with a salmon fillet. Garnish with a sprinkling of sesame seeds, a lime wedge and a cilantro sprig.

Serves 4.

Zucchini Ribbon Salad
2 small zucchini, about ¾ lb (350 g) total
½ small red onion, peeled and cut into thin rings
½ mango, peeled and cut into small dice
½ medium red pepper, seeded and cut into thin
  strips
fresh cilantro, rough chopped, to taste
juice of 1 small lime
2 tbsp (30 mL) sesame oil
¼ cup (50 mL) sweet chilli sauce
sea salt

Using a mandoline, adjust the blades to approximately ⅛ in (2 mm) thickness. Slice zucchini, creating a ribbon or fettuccini shape until centre seeds are reached. Discard centre. Blanch zucchini ribbons in boiling salted water for 30 to 40 seconds or until *al dente*. Strain and cool in ice water. When cool, remove from ice water and lay on towel to dry.

In a bowl combine zucchini, onion, mango, red pepper and cilantro. In a separate bowl whisk together lime juice, sesame oil and sweet chilli sauce. Drizzle over zucchini and gently toss. Adjust seasoning with sea salt.

Gravlax Salad with Papaya Basil Salsa
and Julienne Peppers and Sprouts

Val d'Isère Restaurant, Whistler, BC

The ease with which one can prepare this gravlax recipe from the kitchens of Val d'Isère Restaurant is almost sinful. With a minimum of preparation you are rewarded with delicately flavoured salmon that literally melts in your mouth. Gravlax is traditionally prepared with dill but this recipe is flavoured with juniper berries, giving the finished product a delightful aromatic essence.

Gravlax

1 lb (500 g) BC salmon fillet, with skin
1 tsp (5 mL) coriander seeds
2 tsp (10 mL) juniper berries
3 tbsp (45 mL) coarse sea salt
1 ½ tbsp (22 mL) granulated sugar
1 tsp (5 mL) coarsely ground pepper

Remove bones from salmon and pat dry with paper towel.

Crush coriander and juniper seeds with a mortar and pestle. In a bowl, combine coriander, juniper, salt, sugar and pepper.

Place salmon, skin side down, on a sheet of plastic wrap. Coat flesh side of salmon with salt mixture and press to adhere. Wrap salmon with plastic wrap, making sure it is tightly encased. Place in a shallow dish and refrigerate, turning occasionally, at least 24 hours and up to 2 days.

Remove salmon from wrapping. Rinse under cold water, completely removing salt mixture. Pat dry and refrigerate, unwrapped, 1 hour. Re-wrap with plastic wrap and refrigerate until ready to serve.

Papaya Salsa

2 cups (500 mL) peeled and finely diced papaya
1 ½ to 2 tsp (7 to 10 mL) lemon juice
1 tbsp (15 mL) chopped fresh basil

In a bowl, combine all ingredients and toss, coating papaya with basil. Reserve.

Continued on p. 38

Gravlax Salad with Papaya Basil Salsa and Julienne Peppers and Sprouts (continued)

Julienne Peppers and Sprouts

1 ½ tsp (7 mL) sesame oil
1 medium red pepper, cut in julienne strips
½ green pepper, cut in julienne strips
2 cups (500 mL) mung bean sprouts

Heat sesame oil in a skillet over medium-high heat; add peppers and bean sprouts and sauté until lightly cooked but still crisp.

Ginger Vinaigrette

½ cup white wine
pinch of saffron
1 tbsp (15 mL) fresh lime juice
1 tbsp (15 mL) sherry vinegar
1 tbsp (15 mL) ginger juice*
½ cup (125 mL) extra virgin olive oil
salt and pepper

Heat wine and saffron in a small saucepan over high heat. Bring to a boil and reduce to 2 tbsp (30 mL). Cool.

In a blender, combine wine reduction, lime juice, vinegar and ginger juice; pulse to combine. With blender running, add olive oil in a slow steady stream until emulsified. Adjust seasoning with salt and pepper.

Makes ⅔ cup (175 mL).

*To make ginger juice: finely grate fresh ginger into a small bowl. Press pulp through a fine mesh sieve to extract juice.

To serve: divide julienne vegetables among 4 serving plates. With a sharp knife, thinly slice the salmon on the bias, removing it from the skin. Arrange gravlax on vegetables and top with Papaya Salsa. Drizzle Ginger Vinaigrette around.

Serves 4.

Salmon Salad
Niçoise

Our Salmon Salad Niçoise is similar to the traditional tuna-based Salad Niçoise — composed of tuna, tomatoes, olives, anchovies, hard boiled eggs, green beans and herbs — a signature recipe of Nice, France. This version encompasses all that is beneficial from the renowned Mediterranean diet — fresh fish, fresh vegetables and olive oil.

1 garlic clove, halved
½ lb (225 g) green beans, cooked *al dente*
1 6 oz (175 mL) jar marinated artichoke hearts, drained and quartered
2 tomatoes, cut in wedges
12 oz (350 g) salmon fillet, cooked, cooled and chunked
1 cup (250 mL) kalamata olives
4 anchovy fillets, chopped
Vinaigrette (recipe follows)
romaine and leaf lettuce to serve 4
3 hard cooked eggs, cut in wedges

Rub salad bowl with cut side of garlic clove, and discard garlic. Add beans, artichokes, tomatoes, salmon, olives and anchovies to bowl; drizzle with vinaigrette and gently toss to mix.

To serve: arrange lettuce on serving plates and top with salmon mixture. Garnish with hard cooked eggs.

Serves 4.

Vinaigrette
2 tbsp (30 mL) lemon juice
1 clove garlic, sliced
¼ tsp (1 mL) each, salt, pepper and dry mustard
⅓ cup (75 mL) extra virgin olive oil

Process all ingredients except olive oil in a food processor until blended. With motor running, add olive oil in a slow steady stream processing until emulsified.

Makes ½ cup (125 mL).

Cedar-Planked Salmon, p.54

Entrées

In this section you will find a variety of salmon entrées. You will note that most British Columbian and western chefs specify sockeye, coho or other Pacific salmon species, while chefs from the Atlantic Provinces prefer Atlantic salmon. The salmon in the recipes of this collection is interchangeable. Choose whichever type is available and pleasing to your palate, keeping in mind that freshness is of the utmost importance.

Salmon on a Bed of Pasta
with Spinach Sauce

Little Shemogue Country Inn, Little Shemogue, NB

Tantalize your guests with this eye-catching dish. The subtle flavour of bacon and spinach complement one another in the vibrant sauce, while the salmon is simply enhanced with a little vermouth and fresh lemon juice.

12 oz (375 g) fresh spinach, rinsed
¾ cup (175 mL) heavy cream (35% m.f.)
6 slices lean bacon, diced
1 small onion, diced
2 cloves garlic, minced
salt and pepper
fettuccini to serve 4
4 salmon fillets, 5 oz (140 g) each
2 tbsp (30 mL) dry white vermouth
juice of 1 lemon
4 tbsp (60 mL) butter, shaved
salt and pepper, second amount

Bring a large saucepan of salted water to a boil. Wash spinach and boil 2 minutes. Drain well and place spinach in a blender. Add cream and purée.

In a skillet, over medium-high heat, brown diced bacon and onion until bacon is crisp. Stir in garlic and continue to sauté 1 minute. Transfer with a slotted spoon to a saucepan, stir in spinach mixture and simmer 3 minutes. Adjust seasoning with salt and pepper and keep warm.

Preheat oven to 400° F (200° C). Prepare pasta according to package directions, drain and keep warm.

While pasta is cooking place salmon on a rimmed baking sheet, sprinkle with vermouth, lemon juice and butter shavings. Season with salt and pepper and bake 8 to 10 minutes, depending upon the thickness of the fish.

To serve: arrange pasta on serving plates, drizzle with spinach sauce and top with salmon fillets.

Serves 4.

Maple-Roasted Salmon
with Maple Bourbon Sauce

Horizons Restaurant, Burnaby, BC

Proud of traditional West Coast cuisine, Executive Chef John Garrett of Horizons Restaurant comments: "The legendary Maple Salmon was a favourite at Horizons long before I appeared on the scene. I have modified it slightly over the years, but it is still basically the same recipe." Chef Garrett serves the dish accompanied by skewers of shrimp and a colourful array of crisp vegetables.

1 cup (250 mL) pure maple syrup
1 cup (250 mL) fresh orange juice
2 tbsp (30 mL) fresh lemon juice
1 tsp (5 mL) ground black pepper
2 tbsp (30 mL) liquid honey
4 salmon fillets, 7 oz (200 g) each
2 tbsp (30 mL) butter
Maple Bourbon Sauce (recipe follows)

In a shallow dish combine maple syrup, orange juice, lemon juice, black pepper and honey. Add salmon fillets and turn to coat. Marinate salmon, covered and refrigerated, at least 6 hours. Preheat oven to 400°F (200°C). Heat butter in a large ovenproof skillet over medium-high heat, add salmon and sear 1 minute. Turn fillets and transfer skillet to oven. Bake until fish is just cooked, about 8 minutes.

To serve: pour Maple Bourbon Sauce on warmed plates and top with salmon. Accompany with seasonal vegetables of choice.

Serves 4.

Maple Bourbon Sauce
¾ cup (175 mL) chicken stock
½ cup (125 mL) dry white wine
½ cup (125 mL) heavy cream (35% m.f.)
⅓ cup (75 mL) pure maple syrup
2 tsp (10 mL) bourbon (Jack Daniel's, Wild Turkey, etc.)

Combine chicken stock and white wine in a small pot over high heat; bring to a boil and reduce by half. Lower heat to medium and whisk in heavy cream. Return to a boil and reduce by one third.

Stir in maple syrup and return to a boil. Immediately reduce heat and simmer 20 minutes, stirring occasionally. Remove from heat and let stand 5 minutes. Whisk in bourbon. Serve warm.

Makes 1 cup (250 mL).

Grilled Salmon
with Jicama Citrus Salsa

Stories at Halliburton House Inn, Halifax, NS

In this eye-catching presentation from the Halliburton House Inn, the subtle flavour of salmon is pleasantly complemented by a crisp vegetable and tangy fruit salsa.

2 tbsp (30 mL) fresh lime juice
6 tbsp (90 mL) extra virgin olive oil
1 tbsp (15 mL) light soy sauce
½ cup (125 mL) peeled, julienned jicama
¼ each julienned yellow and red peppers
1 blood orange, peeled, pith removed and sectioned
1 orange, peeled, pith removed and sectioned
1 ruby grapefruit, peeled, pith removed, sectioned and halved
1 tbsp (15 mL) fresh ginger, minced
½ jalapeno pepper, seeded and finely diced
2 tbsp (30 mL) chopped fresh cilantro
4 salmon fillets, 6 oz (170 g) each
salt and pepper

Whisk together the lime juice, oil and soy sauce. Add jicama, peppers, oranges, grapefruit, ginger, jalapeno pepper and cilantro, tossing to combine. Place in a non-reactive bowl and allow flavours to blend at least 1 hour.

Preheat grill to high. Season salmon with salt and pepper and grill, turning once until barely opaque and fish flakes easily.

To serve: divide fillets among serving plates, top with salsa. Accompany with new potatoes or rice pilaf.

Serves 4.

Green-Tea-Rubbed Salmon
with Rice Pilaf and Citrus Relish

Ste. Anne's Resort and Spa, Grafton, ON

Executive Chef Christopher Ennew has created an impressive salmon entrée that features subtle Asian flavours. We have included his recipe for Green Tea Rub but commercial tea rubs may be found in the specialty food section of most supermarkets.

The chef uses purple — also known as black Asian — rice in his pilaf recipe. You will find that this rice requires a longer cooking time than traditional long grain rice.

4 salmon fillets, 6 oz (170 g) each
4 tbsp (60 mL) Green Tea Rub (recipe follows)
Purple Rice Pilaf (recipe follows)
Citrus Relish (recipe follows)

Pat 1 tbsp (15 mL) dry tea rub on one side of each salmon portion. Remove fillets to a baking dish and reserve, covered, at room temperature for 30 minutes.

Preheat oven to 350°F (180°C). Bake fillets until fish flakes and is opaque, about 15 to 18 minutes, depending upon thickness of the fillet.

To serve: place rice pilaf in centre of plates and top with salmon. Portion small amount of citrus relish on the salmon and spoon remaining relish around the rice.

Serves 4 to 6.

Green Tea Rub
1 oz (30 g) loose green tea (16 bags)
1 tsp (5 mL) sea salt
½ tsp (2 mL) ground black pepper
¼ tsp (1 mL) ground coriander
pinch ground cardamom
pinch ground cumin

If loose tea leaves are large, place in a mortar and grind slightly with a pestle. Place all ingredients in a zip-lock bag and shake to combine. Remove amount needed for recipe and store remainder for future use.

Continued on p. 48

Green Tea Rubbed Salmon (continued)

Purple Rice Pilaf

1 tsp (5 mL) olive oil
1 large shallot, chopped
½ cup (125 mL) purple rice
1 ½ cups (375 mL) vegetable stock
pinch ground cardamom
salt and pepper

Heat oil in a saucepan over medium heat. Add shallots and sauté, stirring constantly until softened, about 2 minutes. Add rice, stir and cook 1 minute. Add stock, bring to a boil, cover and reduce heat to low; cook 20 minutes. Remove from heat and rest 10 minutes. Adjust seasoning with cardamom and salt and pepper to taste.

Citrus Relish

2 small limes
1 medium orange
1 large lemon
1 tsp (5 mL) olive oil
1 medium shallot, minced
1 tbsp (15 mL) rice wine vinegar
½ cup (125 mL) apple cider
1 tsp (5 mL) cornstarch
1 tsp (5 mL) chopped cilantro
salt and pepper

Zest the rinds of limes, orange and lemon and place in a bowl. Peel fruit and remove segments being careful to remove all pith; place in bowl with zest.

Heat oil in a saucepan over medium heat; add shallots and cook 1 minute. Deglaze pan with rice wine vinegar and reduce until almost no liquid remains. Add cider and reserved fruit and zest to saucepan and reduce by half.

Mix cornstarch with a little cold water and stir into citrus mixture. Cook 1 minute, remove from heat and add cilantro. Adjust seasoning with salt and pepper to taste. Serve warm.

Poached Atlantic
Salmon

Shaw's Hotel, Brackley Beach, PE

This whole poached salmon is a specialty at Shaw's Hotel. It is easy to prepare and delicious when napped with their White Wine Sauce.

2 ½ to 3 lb (1.25 to 1.5 kg) fresh Atlantic
   salmon
1 cup (250 mL) dry white wine
½ cup (125 mL) lemon juice
6 to 8 peppercorns
1 tsp (5 mL) salt
1 large carrot, peeled and diced
1 medium onion, peeled and sliced
1 large stalk celery with top, sliced
¼ cup (60 mL) chopped fresh tarragon
White Wine Sauce (recipe follows)

Rinse and pat dry salmon; place on a rack in a poaching pan and add enough cold water to cover fish. Add remaining ingredients to pan and bring to a boil. Reduce heat and simmer, covered, 2 minutes per pound of fish. Turn off heat and let stand in water, 1 hour. Carefully remove salmon from pan, remove skin and place fish on a serving platter.

To serve: plate salmon with White Wine Sauce. Accompany with vegetables of choice.

Serves 6.

White Wine Sauce
2 tbsp (30 mL) butter
2 tbsp (30 mL) all-purpose flour
⅔ cup (150 mL) milk
⅓ cup (75 mL) heavy cream (35% m.f.)
2 tbsp (30 mL) dry white wine
salt and white pepper
1 tbsp (15 mL) chopped parsley

In a small saucepan, melt butter and stir in flour to form a roux. Cook until bubbly, 1 to 2 minutes, stirring constantly. Whisk in milk, cream and wine. Cook over medium heat until thickened. Adjust seasoning with salt and pepper and stir in parsley. Serve immediately.

Makes 1 cup (250 mL).

Pan-Seared Medallion of BC Salmon
with Golden Potato, Apple and Dungeness Crab Galette and a Lemon and Rosemary Reduction

The Aerie Resort, Malahat, BC

The Aerie Resort insists that only the freshest of local produce and seafood be served from their kitchen. In this recipe they feature local Pacific salmon and Dungeness crab accompanied by fresh British Columbia ingredients.

Though this recipe is composed of many steps, the chefs at the Aerie feel it is easily prepared in advance and simple to cook and present when guests arrive. The flavours in this entrée complement each other perfectly and will delight your palate.

Salmon

1 lb (500 g) BC salmon fillet
¼ cup (60 mL) soft butter
3 tbsp (45 mL) chopped mixed herbs (parsley, thyme, rosemary)
salt and pepper

Remove skin and all bones from salmon. Lay fillet on a piece of plastic wrap and cover with a second piece of wrap. Gently pound fillet, flattening slightly to make it a uniform thickness.

Lay out a piece of aluminium foil that is longer than the fillet, shiny side down. Spread half the butter on the fillet; top with half the herbs and season with salt and pepper. Place the fillet, butter side down, on the foil and spread the remaining butter and herbs on the exposed fillet. Season with salt and pepper.

Gently roll the fillet, jellyroll-fashion, and seal with the foil. Refrigerate 2 hours.

Galette

3 medium Yukon Gold potatoes, skins on
2 Granny Smith apples
1 medium onion
2 tbsp (30 mL) olive oil
1 tsp (5 mL) honey
4 oz (120 g) Dungeness crab meat
1 tbsp (15 mL) chopped chives
salt and pepper

Blanch potatoes until cooked through, about 12 to 15 minutes. Cool completely and then peel. Peel apples and peel and julienne onion. With a mandoline, julienne potatoes and apple, removing each to separate bowls.

Heat olive oil in a heavy skillet over high heat. When hot, add onion and apples and sauté until golden brown, stirring constantly. Stir in honey, remove from heat and add to potatoes along with the crab and chives. Toss to combine and season with salt and pepper to taste.

Form into 8 patties of equal size, about ½-in (1.25-cm) thick. Reserve, covered.

Continued on p. 52

Continued on p. 52

Pan-Seared Medallion of BC Salmon (continued)

Lemon Rosemary Reduction

2 tbsp (30 mL) olive oil
2 carrots, chopped
1 stalk celery, chopped
2 large shallots, chopped
1 stalk lemon grass, pulverized and chopped
1 cup (250 mL) dry white wine
2 cups (500 mL) fish stock
1 cup (250 mL) chicken stock
2 sprigs rosemary
juice of 1 lemon
salt and pepper

Heat olive oil in a heavy skillet over low heat. Add carrots, celery, shallots and lemon grass, cover and sweat until softened, about 15 minutes.

Add wine, raise heat and reduce by half. Add fish and chicken stock and reduce by three-quarters until liquid becomes syrupy. Reduce heat, add rosemary sprigs and "steep" 5 minutes. Add lemon juice and adjust seasoning with salt and pepper.

Strain mixture through a fine mesh sieve; discard pulp and return liquid to saucepan; keep warm.

To Assemble:

olive oil
rosemary sprigs

Preheat oven to 425°F (220C°).

With a sharp knife, slice rolled salmon fillets into 1-in (2.5-cm) medallions. Heat 2 tbsp (30 mL) olive oil in a skillet over high heat. Place medallions in pan and sear each side for 1 minute. Remove to preheated oven and bake until medium, about 6 minutes.

Heat 2 tbsp (30 mL) olive oil in another skillet over medium-high heat. Place potato rounds in pan and fry until golden, about 2 to 3 minutes on each side. Remove and keep warm.

To serve: on each of 4 warmed plates, creatively arrange 2 potato rounds and 2 salmon medallions. Spoon warm reduction around salmon. Garnish with fresh rosemary.

Serves 4.

Honey Horseradish
Coho Salmon

Nautical Nellies Steak & Seafood House, Victoria, BC

When we tested this recipe we noticed at once the uniqueness of the ingredients! Who would have thought that honey, horseradish and soy sauce could so beautifully complement a salmon fillet? We will let you in on a little secret from Chef Lisa Hartery — the sauce works equally well on steak.

6 coho salmon fillets, 6 oz (170 g) each
⅔ cup (150 mL) liquid honey
⅓ cup (75 mL) creamed horseradish
2 ½ tbsp (37 mL) soy sauce
¼ tsp (1 mL) chilli powder
1 tbsp (15 mL) grainy mustard

Preheat oven to 400°F (200°C). Rinse and pat dry salmon fillets and place on a parchment-lined rimmed baking sheet.

Place remaining ingredients in a bowl and stir to combine. Brush glaze over salmon and bake until fish flakes easily and is opaque, about 10 minutes.

Serves 6.

Cedar-Planked
Salmon

A Snug Harbour Inn, Ucluelet, BC

Use the freshest British Columbia salmon you can find says Sue Brown, owner/chef of A Snug Harbour Inn. This recipe has been handed down through generations of West Coast fishermen and may be prepared either in the oven or on the barbecue grill. If using a grill, adjust the heat so the board does not ignite.

1 untreated cedar plank, slightly larger than the
   size of the fish you wish to cook
¼ cup (60 mL) olive oil
juice of 1 lemon
1 tbsp (15 mL) chopped fresh basil
½ tsp (2 mL) salt
1 tsp (5 mL) freshly ground black pepper
1 salmon fillet, 1 to 2 lb (0.5 to 1 kg)

Soak cedar plank for several hours in room-temperature water. It is a good idea to place something heavy on the plank to be sure that all the wood is submerged and soaked.

In a shallow baking dish, combine all ingredients except the salmon. Add salmon to dish, turn to coat and marinate, covered and refrigerated for several hours.

Preheat oven to 450°F (230°C). Place soaked plank in oven and bake 5 minutes. Remove fish from marinade and place on plank; bake until cooked, about 10 to 12 minutes, depending upon thickness.

Serves 4 to 6.

Salmon in Saor
(Marinated Cold Salmon)

Da Maurizio Dining Room, Halifax, NS

Chef and owner Maurizio Bertossi offers a variation of 'saor,' the traditional Venetian method of preparing fresh fish, usually sardines, layered in onion and flavoured with vinegar. His recipe features sautéed salmon, sweet onion and raisins marinated in a wine, lemon and balsamic vinegar sauce.

We like to accompany this chilled salmon dish with flavoured couscous and asparagus served at room temperature.

6 salmon fillets, 3 oz (85 g) each
¼ cup (60 mL) all-purpose flour
3 tbsp (45 mL) extra virgin olive oil, divided
1 ½ cups (375 mL) thinly sliced sweet onion
½ cup (125 mL) sultana raisins
1 cup (250 mL) white wine
1 tbsp (15 mL) granulated sugar
2 tbsp (30 mL) lemon juice
2 tbsp (30 mL) balsamic vinegar
salt and pepper
lemon slices, as garnish

Dredge salmon fillets in flour to coat. Heat 1 tbsp (15 mL) oil in a skillet over medium-high heat and sauté the fillets until the flesh flakes easily and is opaque. Remove and place on a paper towel to absorb excess cooking oil. Arrange salmon in a shallow serving dish and reserve.

Heat remaining oil in a skillet over medium heat; add onion and sauté until golden, stirring frequently. Add raisins, wine and sugar, raise heat and reduce by half. Stir in lemon juice and vinegar and simmer 1 minute. Adjust seasoning with salt and pepper.

Pour over salmon and chill for 2 hours, basting occasionally.

To serve: portion chilled salmon on plates. Garnish with lemon slices.

Serves 6.

Roasted Spring Salmon
with Rhubarb Compote

Bishop's Restaurant, Vancouver, BC

John Bishop comments that his spring recipe, featuring the first Pacific coast Chinook salmon of the year coupled with rhubarb — spring's earliest vegetable — makes a delightful combination. The compote's sweet and sour flavour provides a great contrast to the rich salmon.

4 spring salmon fillets, 6 oz (170 g) each
salt and pepper
1 tsp (5 mL) vegetable oil
Rhubarb Compote (recipe follows)

Preheat oven to 400°F (200°C) and line a baking sheet with parchment paper.

Season fillets with salt and pepper. Heat oil in a skillet over medium-high heat. Add fillets and sear, on one side only, until golden, about 2 minutes.

Remove fillets, seared side down, to prepared baking sheet. Roast in oven until flesh in centre is opaque, about 5 to 7 minutes.

To serve: place fillets on warmed plates and pour a ring of Rhubarb Compote around the salmon. Accompany with vegetables of choice.

Serves 4.

Rhubarb Compote
1 ½ cups (375 mL) Japanese rice vinegar
½ cup (125 mL) granulated sugar
½ cup (125 mL) diced red onion
1 tsp (5 mL) grated fresh ginger root
1 lb (500 g) rhubarb, cut into 1-in (2.5-cm) slices
salt

Combine vinegar and sugar in a saucepan over medium heat; bring to a simmer, stirring frequently. Add onion, ginger and rhubarb, cover and simmer, stirring occasionally, until soft, about 45 minutes. Remove from heat and allow to cool slightly, about 15 minutes.

Remove rhubarb to a blender or food processor and pulse to break down rhubarb, but do not puree. Adjust seasoning with salt. Cool and refrigerate, covered. Bring to room temperature before serving. Will keep up to 2 weeks in refrigerator.

Wild Coho Risotto with Horseradish,
Lemon And Chives

Pyramid Lake Resort, Jasper, AB

The piquant flavour of lemon married with the bite of horseradish makes this risotto memorable, a dish you will prepare time and again. We served it with a salad of mâche greens, avocado, Campari tomatoes and toasted pine nuts accompanied by Italian bread and a nice glass of Sauvignon Blanc wine — light, lovely and oh-so-good.

1 lb (500 g) wild coho salmon
2 tbsp (30 mL) extra virgin olive oil
½ cup (125 mL) finely diced onion
2 cloves garlic, minced
2 cups (500 mL) arborio rice
½ cup (125 mL) dry white wine
6 to 8 cups (1.5 to 2 L) chicken stock, heated
2 tbsp (30 mL) butter
3 tbsp (45 mL) grated Parmesan cheese
1 ½ tbsp (22 mL) creamed horseradish, or to
    taste
zest of 2 lemons
juice of 1 lemon
2 tbsp (30 mL) chopped chives
salt and white pepper
individual chives for garnish

Remove skin from salmon and discard. Cube salmon into bite-size pieces and reserve.

Heat olive oil in a heavy saucepan over medium-low heat; add onion and garlic and cook, covered, 5 minutes or until softened. Add rice and sauté 2 to 3 minutes or until grains are slightly transparent. Deglaze pan with wine and reduce until almost dry.

Pour in ½ cup (125 mL) warm stock; cook, stirring often and adding remaining stock ½ cup (125 mL) at a time, allowing rice to completely absorb liquid each time, about 30 minutes or until rice is almost tender. Add salmon and continue cooking until fish is just cooked.

Remove from heat and gently stir in butter, Parmesan cheese, horseradish, lemon zest and juice and chopped chives, being careful not to break up salmon. Adjust seasoning with salt and white pepper to taste.

To serve: portion into warmed bowls. Garnish with chives.

Serves 4 to 6.

Apple-Braised Salmon
with Citrus-Spiced Couscous

River House Grill, St. Albert, AB

Easy-to-prepare couscous, a staple of North African cuisine, is often overlooked by North American cooks. In this dish owner/chef Willie White serves his poached salmon and apples on a bed of couscous that he has been prepared with stock and the juice of half a lemon and lime. The natural citrus flavour is a perfect accompaniment to the fish.

1 cup (250 mL) apple cider or apple juice
2 tbsp (30 mL) apple cider vinegar
½ cup (125 mL) canola oil (first amount)
juice of ½ lemon
juice of ½ lime
3 tbsp (45 mL) finely diced onion
1 tsp (5 mL) whole grain mustard
assorted, chopped fresh chives, thyme, tarragon,
   dill and parsley, to taste
4 to 6 salmon fillets, 6 oz (170 g) each
salt and freshly ground pepper to season
1 tbsp (15 mL) canola oil (second amount)
1 ¾ cups (425 mL) water
juice of ½ lemon (second amount)
juice of ½ lime (second amount)
10 oz (280 g) couscous
1 red and 1 green apple, cored and thinly sliced

Blend together the first eight ingredients and let stand several hours to allow the flavours to develop. This poaching liquid will last up to one week refrigerated.

Preheat oven to 400°F (200°C). Rinse and pat dry salmon fillets; season with salt and freshly ground pepper. Heat 1 tbsp (15 mL) oil in an ovenproof skillet over high heat; add salmon fillets and sear one side. Turn fish; gently pour ¾ cup (175 mL) of poaching liquid into skillet and place in oven. Bake until salmon flakes easily and is opaque, about 8 to 10 minutes. Cooking time will depend upon the thickness of the fish. While salmon is baking, prepare couscous. In a saucepan bring water, lemon and lime juice to a boil. Add couscous, stir to combine, cover and remove from heat. Let stand 7 minutes; fluff with a fork.

Bring remaining poaching liquid to a boil, add apple slices and cook until slightly softened, about 1 minute. Drain.

To serve: portion couscous onto serving plates and top with salmon. Garnish with apple slices.

Serves 4 to 6.

Maple-Soya Glazed
Atlantic Salmon

Deerhurst Resort, Huntsville, ON

Choose thick boneless and skinless salmon fillets for this "Rolls Royce" of salmon entrées! At Deerhurst Resort Executive Chef Rory Golden drizzles a little of the glaze around the salmon and accompanies the fish with seasonal vegetables.

1 tbsp (15 mL) canola oil
1 medium shallot, diced
1 tsp (5 mL) finely diced fresh ginger
1 clove garlic, finely diced
1 tbsp (15 mL) teriyaki sauce
1 cup (250 mL) pure maple syrup
2 tsp (10 mL) fresh lemon juice
4 to 6 salmon fillets, 6 oz (170 g) each

Heat oil over medium heat in a small saucepan. Add shallots, garlic and ginger and sauté, stirring frequently until tender, being careful not to brown. Add teriyaki sauce, maple syrup and lemon juice, raise heat to medium-high and boil until reduced by one-third. Remove from heat and cool.

Preheat oven to 350°F (180°C). Divide maple glaze: pour half into a shallow dish and gently reheat remainder on stovetop. Add salmon fillets to glaze in shallow dish; coat one side and then flip to coat other side, rest in marinade 5 minutes.

Remove fillets to a baking dish, discard marinade and bake 10 minutes. Brush salmon with the warmed maple glaze, return to oven and continue to bake until fish flakes and is opaque, about 5 to 7 minutes longer, depending upon thickness of the fillet. Remove from oven and brush again with maple glaze.

To serve: place salmon on warmed plates and drizzle remaining glaze around fillets. Accompany with rice or potatoes and seasonal vegetables of choice.

Serves 4 to 6.

Salmon
Brûlée

Vineland Estates Winery, Vineland, ON

In preparing haute cuisine dishes you sometimes risk losing the basic flavours you are trying to enhance. Chef Mark Picone at Vineland Estates restaurant feels the quality of his ingredients speak for themselves, hence the utter simplicity of this dish. Optimum freshness is paramount!

4 salmon fillets, 6 oz (170 g) each, boneless with skin on
½ tsp (2 mL) Fleur de Sel or other high grade-sea salt
1 tsp (5 mL) seasoning of your preference: lemon-thyme, citrus peel, pepper, etc.
2 tbsp (30 mL) extra virgin olive oil, portioned
1 lemon, sliced into wedges

Sprinkle flesh side of salmon portions with salt and your choice of seasoning. Heat a thick-bottomed skillet until hot but not smoking. Add 1 ½ tablespoon (22 mL) oil and immediately place salmon, flesh side down, in the pan; cook 2 minutes. Turn fish, reduce heat to medium and cook until skin is crisp and fish is opaque, flaking easily with a fork.

To serve: gently lift fillets and place, skin side down, on a bed of your favourite roasted seasonal vegetables. Garnish with lemon wedges and a sprinkle of olive oil.

Serves 4.

Inn on the Twenty
Atlantic Salmon

Inn on the Twenty, Jordan, ON

Atlantic salmon is frequently featured on Executive Chef Kevin Maniaci's menus at this highly rated restaurant. In his recipe the subtle flavour of salmon is complemented, but not overwhelmed, by the addition of fresh dill and chives.

1 ½ lb (725 g) boneless salmon, skin on
salt and pepper
2 tbsp (30 mL) fresh dill weed, chopped
8 chives, chopped
1 ½ tbsp (22 mL) vegetable oil
2 tbsp (30 mL) butter
6 tbsp (90 mL) white wine

Season salmon with salt and pepper, and sprinkle with dill and chives. Preheat a heavy-bottomed skillet over medium-high heat; add oil and butter and bring to a smoking point. Place salmon, flesh side down, in pan and sear 3 minutes. Turn fish, add wine and deglaze skillet, about 2 minutes.

Cover pan, remove from burner and let stand until fish is opaque and flakes easily when tested with a fork, about 5 to 7 minutes.

Serves 4.

Salmon and Spinach
Lasagna

Dufferin Inn & San Martello Dining Room, Saint John, NB

We love recipes that can be prepared in advance and simply popped in the oven when guests arrive. This appetizing salmon lasagna, a creation of chef/owner Axel Begner of the Dufferin Inn substitutes a creamy béchamel sauce for the traditional tomato sauce found in Italian lasagna. Serve it with a Caesar salad and warm garlic bread.

Béchamel Sauce (recipe follows)
1 lb (500 g) fresh spinach, stems removed and
   rinsed
8 oz (250 g) lasagna pasta sheets
1 ¼ lb (620 g) skinless salmon fillet, cut in ½-in
   (1-cm) slices
salt and pepper
¼ cup (60 mL) freshly grated Parmesan cheese
4 oz (125 g) mozzarella cheese, grated
chopped fresh dill

Preheat oven to 350°F (180°C). Prepare béchamel sauce, reserve and keep warm.

Blanch spinach in boiling salted water, 1 minute, drain and press firmly to remove water. Prepare lasagna sheets following manufacturer's directions, drain.

In a greased 8 x 10-in (20 x 25-cm) baking pan, spread a layer of béchamel sauce. Add a layer of pasta sheets, top with a layer of salmon and a layer of spinach. Repeat with sauce, pasta, salmon and spinach ending with a layer of sauce. Top with Parmesan and mozzarella cheese. Remove to oven and bake 40 to 50 minutes, until top is browned and lasagna is bubbly. Sprinkle with dill.

Serves 4.

Béchamel Sauce (supplied by authors)
2 tbsp (30 mL) butter
2 tbsp (30 mL) flour
2 cups (500 mL) milk
½ tsp (2 mL) salt
¼ tsp (1 mL) white pepper
pinch of ground nutmeg (optional)
2 egg yolks

In a large saucepan melt butter over medium heat; whisk in flour; cook, without browning, about 3 minutes. Gradually whisk in milk and bring to a boil, stirring constantly. Stir in salt, pepper and nutmeg. In a small bowl, beat egg yolks lightly and stir in a little of the hot mixture. Blend thoroughly, and then stir back into the saucepan. Continue to cook sauce, stirring constantly until thickened.

Confit of Salmon
on Red Wine Spinach Risotto

Wellington Court Restaurant, St. Catharines, ON

While any species of salmon may be used in this recipe, Chef Erik Peacock of Wellington Court Restaurant prefers wild British Columbia salmon. He serves the salmon atop the risotto accompanied by seasonal vegetables.

Chef Peacock comments that the cooking time for both the salmon and risotto are the same, approximately 25 minutes.

2 cups (500 mL) olive oil
4 salmon fillets, 6 oz (170 g) each
4 cups (1 L) low-sodium chicken broth
1 small onion, minced
2 tbsp (30 mL) butter
1 cup (250 mL) arborio rice
1 cup (250 mL) dry red wine
1 ½ cups (375 mL) baby spinach, stems removed
1 cup (250 mL) grated parmigiano-reggiano
　cheese
salt and freshly ground pepper

Preheat oven to 200° F (100° C).

Pour olive oil in a large heavy-bottomed ovenproof skillet and warm over very low heat until the oil reaches 200°F (100°C) on an instant-read thermometer.

Carefully submerge salmon in olive oil and remove to oven. Poach salmon for approximately 25 minutes, or until fish is opaque.

While salmon is poaching prepare risotto. Heat chicken broth in a medium saucepan and keep warm. Melt butter in a separate pan over medium-high heat; add onion and sauté, stirring constantly, until softened, about 4 minutes. Add rice and stir for one minute to evenly coat.

Pour in wine and cook, stirring often, until liquid is absorbed. Add stock half a cup (125 mL) at a time, allowing rice to completely absorb liquid before adding more. Continue adding liquid in this fashion until rice is almost cooked, about 20 minutes. Add spinach and cheese, stir and cook 5 minutes longer or until rice is *al dente*. Adjust seasoning with salt and pepper.

Drain salmon and season with coarse salt.

To serve: divide risotto between 4 plates and top with salmon.

Serves 4.

Pan-Roasted Salmon
with Balsamic Maple Glaze on Parsnip Purée

Restaurant Les Fougères, Chelsea, QC

This recipe, the creation of owner/chef Charles Part, is packed with bold flavours. The salmon is seared, then finished off in the oven with a glaze that is a magnificent blend of sweet maple syrup and sour balsamic vinegar. The parsnip purée, with its hint of nutmeg and orange, will introduce you to a delightful new way to serve this tangy root vegetable.

Balsamic vinegar is like wine – you get what you pay for. We suggest buying the finest quality balsamic vinegar that your budget will accommodate.

1 cup (250 mL) pure maple syrup
1 cup (250 mL) balsamic vinegar
6 Atlantic salmon fillets, 6 oz (170 g) each
all-purpose flour seasoned with salt and pepper,
  for dredging
1 tbsp (15 mL) vegetable oil
1 tbsp (15 mL) butter
Parsnip Purée (recipe follows)

Preheat oven to 375°F (190°C).

In a saucepan over medium heat bring maple syrup and vinegar to a boil. Lower heat and simmer until reduced by half and thickened to a syrupy consistency. Set aside and keep warm.

Coat salmon lightly in seasoned flour, shaking off any excess. Heat oil and butter in an ovenproof skillet over medium-high heat; add salmon fillets and sear on both sides. Remove to oven and bake until opaque and fillets flake easily, about 8 minutes. Brush salmon with warm glaze.

To serve: spoon Parsnip Purée on plates and top with salmon. Garnish with an extra drizzle of glaze.

Serves 6.

Parsnip Purée

2 lb (1 kg) parsnips, peeled and sliced
½ cup (125 mL) butter
¼ cup (60 mL) heavy cream (35% m.f.)
¼ cup (60 mL) dry sherry
zest of half an orange
pinch of freshly grated nutmeg
salt and pepper

Combine parsnips and water to cover in a
saucepan. Bring to a boil; reduce heat to
simmer, cover and cook until parsnips are soft;
drain. In a food processor, add parsnips and
process until very smooth. Add butter, cream,
sherry, orange zest and nutmeg and pulse to
combine. Adjust seasoning with salt and pepper.

Salmon Roulade
with Dill Sauce

Marshlands Inn, Sackville, NB

This recipe is an excellent choice for an elegant dinner party. Prepare your salmon in advance and refrigerate up to 3 hours before baking. For the best result, we suggest that the dill sauce be made just prior to serving.

4 salmon fillets, boneless and skinless, 4 to 5 oz
   (120 to 140g) each
5 oz (140 g) fresh spinach
8 oz (250 g) button mushrooms
2 tbsp (30 mL) butter
1 ½ tbsp (22 mL) heavy cream (35% m.f.)
salt and pepper
Dill Sauce (recipe follows)

Preheat oven to 400°F (200°C).

Lay fillets on a piece of plastic wrap and cover with a second piece of wrap. Gently pound fillets, one at a time, to a size of approximately 8-in (20-cm) square.

Remove stems from spinach and blanch 20 seconds in boiling salted water. Immediately refresh with ice water and drain. Squeeze dry and place on paper towel to dry.

Clean mushrooms and grate with a cheese grater. Melt butter in a small saucepan over medium heat; add mushrooms and sauté until liquid has evaporated, being careful not to brown. Add cream and continue cooking until slightly reduced. Adjust seasoning with salt and pepper and set aside to cool.

To prepare roulade: lay one salmon fillet flat and remove top piece of plastic wrap. Cover salmon with a layer of spinach leaves, and top with a thin layer of mushroom mixture. Gently roll the fillet jellyroll-fashion and place on a piece of foil that has been brushed with butter and sprinkled with salt and pepper. Seal packets and twist ends to form a uniform shape. Repeat procedure with remaining fillets.

Place salmon packets on a baking sheet, remove to oven and bake 18 to 20 minutes.

To serve: remove salmon from foil and slice on an angle with a sharp serrated knife. Portion Dill Sauce between four plates and top with salmon slices. Accompany with rice pilaf and seasonal vegetables of choice.

Serves 4.

Dill Sauce
½ cup (125 mL) white wine
½ cup (125 mL) heavy cream (35% m.f.)
½ cup (125 mL) butter, cubed
1 ½ tbsp (22 mL) chopped fresh dill
salt and pepper

Place wine in a small saucepan over medium high heat and reduce by half. Add cream and reduce by half. Whisk in butter, a few cubes at a time, add dill and season with salt and pepper. Serve immediately.

Fillet Of Salmon
with Cream Leek Sauce

The Quaco Inn, St. Martins, NB

The Quaco Inn, with its close proximity to the Bay of Fundy, always features Atlantic salmon on the menu. This special entrée is a signature dish.

3 tbsp (45 mL) butter
2 green onions, cut into thin 3-in (7.5-cm) julienne strips
1 leek, white part only, cut into thin 3-in (7.5-cm) julienne strips
⅔ cup (150 mL) fish stock
1 cup (250 mL) heavy cream (35% m.f.)
1 ½ tbsp (22 mL) dry vermouth
salt and pepper, to taste
pinch of cayenne pepper
4 salmon fillets, 5 oz (140 g) each
fresh dill sprigs, for garnish

Heat butter in a skillet over medium heat; add green onions and leeks and sauté, stirring frequently, until softened, about 2 minutes. Add fish stock and cook until vegetables are tender. Add cream and simmer until mixture begins to thicken, about 8 minutes. Add vermouth and simmer gently, 5 minutes. Adjust seasoning with salt, pepper and cayenne.

Preheat grill to high. Rinse and pat dry salmon fillets. Place salmon on grill 3 in (8 cm) from heat source and cook, turning once, 5 minutes or until salmon flakes easily and is opaque.

To serve: place fillets on plates and nap with sauce. Garnish with a sprig of fresh dill. Accompany with vegetables of choice.

Serves 4.

Highland
Salmon

Inn on the Cove and Spa, Saint John, NB

Innkeeper Ross Mavis tells us that this marinade will enhance but not mask the wonderful flavour of Atlantic salmon. The recipe has been featured on Tide's Table, a Maritime television cooking show filmed at the inn.

4 Atlantic salmon fillets, 6 oz (170 g) each
½ cup (125 mL) orange juice
zest of one orange
⅓ cup (75 mL) whisky or rye
1 ½ tbsp (22 mL) maple syrup
1 tbsp (15 mL) grainy Dijon mustard
2 tsp (10 mL) Worcestershire sauce
1 tsp (5 mL) black pepper
¾ tsp (4 mL) salt
4 green onions, chopped
2 tsp (10 mL) butter
orange slices, for garnish

Place salmon fillets in a shallow glass baking dish. In a bowl, whisk together orange juice and zest, whisky, maple syrup, mustard, Worcestershire sauce, salt and pepper; pour over salmon. Refrigerate 2 to 4 hours, turning fish at least once.

Preheat grill to high. Remove salmon from marinade, place on grill and cook about 4 minutes on each side, until opaque and flesh flakes easily with a fork. Baste with marinade during last few minutes of cooking.

Meanwhile, heat butter in a small skillet over medium heat, add green onion and sauté until just heated through. Reserve and keep warm.

To serve: portion fillets on plates. Garnish with sautéed green onions and orange slices.

Serves 4.

Atlantic Salmon on Prince Edward Island
Garlic Potato Mash

Dalvay by the Sea, Dalvay, PE

The chefs at Dalvay pride themselves in using fresh local produce, and this recipe featuring Island potatoes and fresh off-the-vine tomatoes is a classic example of their expertise.

2 tbsp (30 mL) olive oil
4 salmon fillets, 6 oz (170 g) each
chopped chives, for garnish
Garlic Potato Mash (recipe follows)
Herb Baked Tomatoes and Crispy Prosciutto
  (recipe follows)
extra virgin olive oil
fresh chopped chives

Preheat oven to 400°F (200°C).

Heat olive oil in an ovenproof skillet over high heat. Add salmon fillets and cook for 2 minutes per side. Remove to oven and bake 5 to 7 minutes until cooked.

To serve: portion potato on plates and place salmon fillets on top. Add tomatoes and prosciutto around the plate. Garnish with a sprinkling of extra virgin olive oil and chopped chives.

Serves 4.

Garlic Potato Mash
4 baking potatoes
salt and pepper
2 cloves garlic, minced
½ cup (125 mL) light cream (10 m.f.)
¼ lb (120 g) butter

Peel potatoes and cut into uniform pieces. Place in a saucepan and cover with water; add a pinch of salt, pepper and the minced garlic. Bring to a boil then simmer until potatoes are cooked through. Drain and mash. Heat cream and butter and whip into potatoes. Reserve and keep warm.

Herb-Baked Tomatoes and Crispy Prosciutto

8 small tomatoes
3 tbsp (45 mL) extra virgin olive oil
1 garlic clove, minced
1 tbsp (15 mL) chopped fresh basil
1 tbsp (15 mL) chopped fresh oregano
12 slices prosciutto

Preheat oven to 400°F (200°C).

Plunge tomatoes into boiling water for 20 seconds to blanch, then directly into a bowl of ice water. After tomatoes have cooled, peel and toss in olive oil, garlic, basil and oregano. Place tomatoes on a baking sheet and bake 10 minutes.

After tomatoes have baked for 3 minutes add prosciutto to baking sheet and bake until crispy, about 7 minutes.

Cumin-Crusted Salmon
with Roast Corn Polenta and Basil Pea Broth

Inn at Bay Fortune, Bay Fortune, PE

The chefs at Inn at Bay Fortune always apply their culinary expertise and creativity in an innovative manner. Their treatment of this complete, three recipe entrée is no exception; the flavours are tantalizingly subtle and the presentation is impressive.

Cumin-Crusted Salmon
6 salmon tournedos, 6 oz (170 g) each
1 cup (250 mL) cornmeal
1 tsp (5 mL) paprika
1 tbsp (15 mL) ground cumin
2 tsp (10 mL) salt
1 tsp (5 mL) freshly ground black pepper
2 tbsp (30 mL) butter
Basil Pea Broth (recipe follows)
Roast Corn Polenta (recipe follows)

Preheat oven to 400°F (200°C). Carefully skin and debone salmon steaks and form into a round. Secure with a toothpick.

Combine cornmeal, paprika, cumin, salt and pepper in a shallow dish. Dredge top of salmon in corn meal mixture to coat evenly. Heat a heavy ovenproof skillet over high heat; add butter and salmon. Brown on corn meal side, about 1 minute, turn and finish cooking in oven for 8 to 10 minutes, until fish flakes easily and is opaque.

To serve: centre Roast Corn Polenta on plate, top with crusted salmon and pour Basil Pea Broth around. Accompany with vegetables of choice.

Serves 6.

Basil Pea Broth
1 ½ cups (375 mL) carrot juice
2 tsp (10 mL) cornstarch
1 cup (250 mL) peas
salt and pepper
½ cup (125 mL) chopped fresh basil

In a small saucepan heat carrot juice. Dilute cornstarch in a small amount of cold water and whisk into juice; cook and stir until sauce is lightly thickened. Add peas and simmer until tender. Adjust seasoning with salt and pepper and stir in basil. Keep warm.

Roast Corn Polenta

½ cup (125 mL) butter
1 onion, diced
4 cups (1 L) corn kernels
4 cups (1 L) milk
½ cup (125 mL) chopped fresh parsley
½ tsp (2 mL) salt
¼ tsp (1 mL) black pepper
2 cups (500 mL) corn meal

Melt butter in a heavy-bottomed saucepan over low heat; add onion, cover and sweat until softened, about 8 minutes. Raise heat to medium, add corn and cook until tender. Whisk in milk, parsley, salt and pepper and bring to a simmer.

Whisking vigorously, add cornmeal in a steady stream until fully incorporated. Change to a wooden spoon and continue stirring until polenta pulls away from the sides of the pan, about 10 minutes.

Roll polenta, between two sheets of plastic wrap to a thickness of ½ in (1 cm). Remove top sheet of plastic wrap and with a biscuit cutter cut polenta into 6 rounds.

Grilled Salmon
with Red Beet Coulis

Sweet Basil Bistro, Halifax, NS

Ruby-red beets, fresh orange segments and zest, good quality balsamic vinegar — a marriage made in heaven! In this dish the chef sears, then finishes his salmon fillet in an oven, allowing the natural flavours to emerge. The punch, both in flavour and presentation, comes from the colourful beet coulis. So simple, so yummy.

¼ cup (60 mL) granulated sugar
1 small orange, peeled, pith removed and
  segmented
½ cup (125 mL) red wine vinegar
2 tbsp (30 mL) balsamic vinegar
3 tbsp (45 mL) butter
¾ cup (175 mL) cooked beets
4 salmon fillets, 6 oz (170 g) each

Heat sugar in a small skillet over medium heat, stirring constantly. When sugar just begins to melt, add orange pieces and vinegars. Place mixture in a blender; add butter and purée. Add beets and purée until smooth. Keep warm.

Preheat oven to 350°F (180°C). Sear salmon on a hot grill, turning once. Remove to oven and bake 6 to 7 minutes, until fish is opaque and flakes easily with a fork.

To serve: plate salmon and decoratively swirl Red Beet Coulis. Accompany with new potatoes and vegetables of choice.

Serves 4.

Blackened Salmon
with Butter Sauce

Inn on the Lake, Waverley, NS

Cajun or Creole cuisine is well known for its blackened seafood and meat recipes, seasoned with Cajun spice and cooked over very high heat. These dishes are hot and crunchy on the outside, succulent and moist on the inside.

'The hotter the better' is often the motto with blackened dishes but the chefs at Inn on the Lake feel the heat intensity is better left in the medium range. Use a commercial Cajun spice of your choice in this recipe remembering that it is the percentage of cayenne pepper that gives the heat.

6 salmon fillets 6 oz (170 g) each
2 tbsp (30 mL) Cajun spices
2 tbsp (30 mL) vegetable oil
3 tbsp (45 mL) white wine
¼ tsp (1 mL) black peppercorns
¼ tsp (1 mL) rosemary
3 tbsp (45 mL) heavy cream (35% m.f.)
½ lb (250 g) unsalted butter
lemon and lime slices, for garnish
fresh parsley, for garnish

Preheat oven to 350°F (180°C). Roll salmon in Cajun spices until well covered. Heat oil in a heavy-bottomed frying pan until very hot. Add salmon, serving side down and sear, turning once. Remove salmon to oven and bake until flesh is opaque, about 5 to 8 minutes. Cooking time will depend upon the thickness of the fish.

Place wine, peppercorns and rosemary in a small saucepan over medium heat, reduce by half. Add cream and reduce until thickened. Cut butter into cubes and add to cream, a few pieces at a time, whisking to blend. Strain.

To serve: spoon sauce over salmon. Garnish with lemon and lime slices and parsley.

Serves 6.

Salmone al Cappuccio
(Salmon Wrapped in Cabbage with Seafood Sauce)

La Perla, Dartmouth, NS

The chef of La Perla takes great care in food presentation and these colourful bundles of seafood are an example of his artistry.

8 red cabbage leaves
4 salmon fillets, 4 to 5 oz (120 to 140 g) each
2 tbsp (30 mL) olive oil
3 tbsp (45 mL) garlic butter
4 oz (120 g) shrimp, peeled, deveined and
   roughly chopped
4 oz (120 g) scallops, roughly chopped
4 oz (120 g) fresh lobster, roughly chopped
⅓ cup (75 mL) dry sherry
1 ½ cups (375 mL) heavy cream (35% m.f.)
salt and pepper
dash paprika
4 cooked lobster claws, optional

Preheat oven to 350°F (180°C).

Blanch cabbage leaves in boiling salted water until tender and pliable. Cool in ice water. Pat dry, then wrap around salmon.

Heat olive oil in a large skillet over medium-high heat; add cabbage-salmon bundles and sauté 2 minutes per side. Remove to oven and bake 8 to 10 minutes, depending upon thickness.

In a medium skillet over high heat melt garlic butter, add seafood and sauté 2 minutes. Add sherry and deglaze pan; add cream and reduce until thickened. Adjust seasoning with salt and pepper.

To serve: portion sauce in deep plates, top with salmon and sprinkle with paprika. Garnish with lobster claw, if desired.

Serves 4.

Honey Mustard
Glazed Salmon

This salmon entrée is sweet, yet it has a definite bite. The glaze is equally tasty as a dipping sauce for shrimp and scallops.

2 tbsp (30 mL) finely chopped onion
⅔ cup (150 mL) whole grain Dijon-style mustard
½ cup (125 mL) liquid honey
6 salmon steaks or fillets, 6 oz (170 g) each
¼ cup (60 mL) all-purpose flour
salt and pepper
1 to 2 tbsp (15 to 30 mL) vegetable oil

Preheat oven to 350°F (180°C).

In a small saucepan combine onion, mustard and honey and cook over low heat, stirring frequently until onion is cooked. Reserve and keep warm.

Lightly dust the salmon with flour and season with salt and pepper. Heat oil in a heavy ovenproof skillet over high heat; add salmon and sear 2 minutes per side. Remove to oven and bake 5 minutes. Remove skillet from oven.

Turn oven to broil. Pour glaze over salmon and broil until brown and bubbly, about 1 minute.

To serve: plate salmon. Accompany with seasonal vegetables of choice.

Serves 6.

Salmon with Leek Straw
and Mango and Orange Salsa

The Dunes Café and Gardens, Brackley Beach, PE

The magnificent gardens of the Dunes Café provide fresh flowers and herbs for use in the restaurant. Not only is their salmon dish delicious, but artistically presented on unique pottery made on site by award-winning potters Peter Janson and Joel Mills. Many patrons purchase these beautiful pieces, which are available in the adjacent gallery and gift shop.

2 leeks, white part only
1 tbsp (15 mL) cornstarch
3 tbsp (45 mL) oil
1 mango, peeled and diced
1 orange, peeled, pith removed and diced
1 red pepper, diced
1 small red onion, diced
2 tbsp chopped cilantro
1 tbsp (15 mL) balsamic vinegar
salt and pepper
4 salmon fillets, 6 oz (170 g) each

Peel off outer layers of leeks and rinse thoroughly; reserve only the white parts. Slice into 3-in (7.5 cm) long julienne strips and dust with cornstarch. Heat oil in a small skillet over medium-high heat; immerse leeks and cook until golden brown. Remove leeks from oil with a slotted spoon and place on paper towel to drain.

In a bowl, combine mango, orange, red pepper and onion; stir in cilantro, vinegar and salt and pepper. Reserve salsa, allowing flavours to blend.

Preheat oven to 350°F (180°C). Heat grill to high.

Grill salmon 1 minute per side, allowing grill marks to form on flesh. Transfer fillets to a baking dish and place in oven. Bake until fish is opaque and flakes easily with a fork, about 8 minutes.

To serve: portion leeks on serving plates, top with salmon and serve salsa on side. Accompany with rice and vegetables of choice.

Serves 4.

Salmon Loaf
with Parsley Egg Sauce

Both fresh and tinned salmon work equally well in this flavourful "comfort food" dish. If using tinned salmon, be sure to drain and remove all skin and bones.

2 cups (500 mL) cooked fresh or tinned salmon, flaked
2 tbsp (30 mL) lemon juice
¾ tsp (4 mL) salt
2 green onions, chopped
2 cups (500 mL) soft bread crumbs
2 eggs, beaten
½ cup (125 mL) mayonnaise
¼ cup (60 mL) whole milk (3.5 % m.f.)
Parsley Egg Sauce (recipe follows)

Preheat oven to 350° F (180° C). In a bowl gently combine all ingredients. Pour into a buttered 6-cup (1.5-L) loaf pan or bundt pan.

Bake 35 minutes until golden on top. Unmold loaf and slice.

To serve: portion loaf on plates and top with Parsley Egg Sauce. Accompany with salad and rice pilaf.

Serves 4 to 6.

Parsley Egg Sauce
1 ½ tbsp (22 mL) butter
1 ½ tbsp (22 mL) all-purpose flour
1 cup (250 mL) whole milk (3.5 % m.f.), scalded
1 egg, hard boiled and finely diced
2 tbsp (30 mL) fresh chopped parsley
salt and white pepper

In a saucepan melt butter over medium heat; whisk in flour stirring constantly, cook 2 minutes. Whisk in milk and bring to a boil. Reduce heat and simmer until sauce has thickened. Fold egg and parsley into sauce; adjust seasoning with salt and pepper.

Makes 1 cup (250 mL).

Index

Library and Archives Canada Cataloguing in Publication

Elliot, Elaine, 1939-
    Salmon : recipes from Canada's best chefs / Elaine Elliot and Virginia Lee. — 2nd ed.

(Flavours series)
Includes index.
ISBN 978-0-88780-726-8

    1. Cookery (Salmon). I. Lee, Virginia, 1947- II. Title. III. Series.

TX748.S24E55 2007   641.6'92   C2007-903106-4

Photo Credits

All photographs by Tammy Fancy with the exception of the following:
Meghan Collins: 2, 49, 53, 54, 57, 64, 65, 71, 74, 83, 87, 88; ACART
Communications Inc. (Source: Department of Fisheries and Oceans): 5-7; Elena
Elisseeva: 60; Formac Publishing Company: 35, 92; Steven Isleifson: 3, 13, 17, 67, 73,
75, 77, 79, 81, 82, 85, 86, 89, 90, 93; Alanna Jankov: 14, 25, 39, 48; Janet Kimber:
31, 45, 56, 78; Alexandru Lamba: 21; Robert Lerich: 9; Suzannah Skelton: 61